Read & Respo

FOR
KS1

Read & Respond

FOR KS1

Author: Sara Stanley

Development Editor: Simret Brar

Editor: Roanne Charles

Assistant Editor: Margaret Eaton

Series Designer: Anna Oliwa

Designer: Liz Gilbert

Illustrations: Janet Ahlberg/Shelagh McNicholas

Text © 2009, Sara Stanley © 2009 Scholastic Ltd

Designed using Adobe InDesign

Published by Scholastic Ltd, Villiers House,
Clarendon Avenue, Leamington Spa,
Warwickshire CV32 5PR

www.scholastic.co.uk

Printed by Bell & Bain

1 2 3 4 5 6 7 8 9   9 0 1 2 3 4 5 6 7 8

British Library Cataloguing-in-Publication Data
A catalogue record for this book is available from the British Library.

ISBN 978-1407-11238-1

Acknowledgements

The publishers gratefully acknowledge permission to reproduce the
following copyright material: **Penguin Group UK** for the use of text
and illustrations from *Burglar Bill* by Janet and Allan Ahlberg, text and
illustrations © 1977, Janet and Allan Ahlberg (1999, Puffin Books).

Every effort has been made to trace copyright holders for the works
reproduced in this book, and the publishers apologise for any inadvertent
omissions.

Burglar Bill

About the book

Burglar Bill leads a cosy life. His house is well equipped with all the necessities: beans, arrowroot biscuits and even hairnets! But all these items have been acquired somewhat illegally for Bill is, as his name indicates, a thief! He steals what he needs, or what he fancies, without much thought for his victims. That is, until one day he steals more than he bargained for in the form of a wailing baby! The situation is happily resolved, however, on the night when the baby's mother, Burglar Betty, decides to burgle Bill's house. The two burglars are forced to face up to the consequences of their behaviour and they both end up as reformed characters.

Burglar Bill introduces one of the most instantly recognisable villains in children's literature. The jovial face, eye mask, burglar stripes and swag bag are the embodiment of the catchphrase 'That's a nice... I'll have that!'

The plot and themes of the book follow the traditions of moral tales for children in which characters get their comeuppance and through it see the error of their ways. Janet Ahlberg's charming illustrations encourage children to 'read' the pictures and deepen and embellish the story lines. In her detailed illustrations throughout this book we see several examples of atmospheric settings and the skilful capture of character.

Burglar Bill offers many opportunities for classroom discussions based on the themes of society, stereotypes and our ideas of right and wrong. As well as providing patterned vocabulary, the language lends itself to the analysis of character, setting, plot and theme. The use of repetitive phrases and dialect draws us into an empathic understanding of Bill, Betty and, indeed, the poor baby! The language lends itself perfectly to enhanced storytelling and drama.

Burglar Bill is just one of a long string of classic picture books by Janet and Allan Ahlberg. It should encourage children to explore the wide range of genres produced by the authors – including poetry, picture books and other fiction as well as novels for older children.

About the authors

Janet and Allan Ahlberg met at teacher-training college in Sunderland and married in 1969.

The couple worked together on many books for children, Allan writing and Janet illustrating, until Janet's untimely death in 1994. They were a perfect partnership, combining words and pictures in a package of more than 37 collaborations. Translated into 21 languages, many of their books have become children's classics, selling millions of copies around the world (see box below for a list of the awards that some of their books have won since they were first published).

Although Allan's dream was always to be a writer, he had many other jobs before he succeeded in fulfilling that early ambition – including teacher, postman, plumber's mate and gravedigger! He has now written over 100 books in total.

Facts, figures and awards
Burglar Bill was first published by Heinemann Ltd in 1977. First published by Puffin Books in paperback in 1999.
Each Peach Pear Plum won the Kate Greenaway Medal in 1978.
In 1986, *The Jolly Postman* won the Kate Greenaway Medal and the Kurt Maschler Award. It was also the winner of the Children's Book Award in 1987.
Peepo! won the Best Books for Babies Award in 1985.
It Was a Dark and Stormy Night was shortlisted for the Sheffield Children's Book Award in 1994.

Cover and title page

Display the cover and invite the children to tell you what they see. What sort of a character do they think Burglar Bill is? What clues does the cover provide? Ask the children to think about why he is smiling.

Point out the title and authors' names. What do the children notice about the letters here? Draw attention to the use of capital letters. Look at the ampersand and ask the children if they know what it means. You may wish to show some other ways to write an ampersand.

Now show the title page. Here we see Burglar Bill in action. Ask the children to comment on how he is dressed and why he has a sack and a torch.

Discuss whether the cover and title page have given any pictorial clues as to what may happen in the story.

Spread 1, Burglar Bill lives by himself...

Read the text, placing some emphasis on the repeated consonant blend 'st'. Ask the children which words come across strongest, and why.

Now focus on the two illustrations across the spread. What contrasts and comparisons can the children make? They might notice the use of stripes, spots and pattern, the windows showing day and night. Look closely at the detail: which items do they think Bill might have stolen?

Spread 2, One night Burglar Bill...

First point out the layout of the illustrations and ask why they might be presented in this way. Discuss how comic strips tell a story without many words. Ask the children to discuss the illustration sequence in pairs and then share their interpretations with the group. Now read

the text, giving Bill a suitable, perhaps Cockney, accent. Comment on similarities of the text to the children's interpretations of the pictures.

Play the 'I'll have that' game. Ask a child to act out creeping through a window and say 'That's a nice... [object] ...I'll have that.' Encourage the actor to give Bill an appropriate voice. The group have to guess what room Bill is entering. Alternatively, the children might like to invent strange items that could be found in a given room. Challenge them to think of the strangest or most unusual objects they can.

Spread 3, When he comes to the sixteenth house...

Read the text on the left-hand page. Point out the addition to Bill's catchphrase 'That's a nice...' in the form of the descriptive adjectives already used in the narration: 'That's a *nice big brown* box *with little holes in it.*' Ask the children to look at some of the other stolen objects in the illustrations and see if they can enhance the catchphrase in the same way. You could start them off with the example: 'That's a nice toothbrush *with prickly bristles on it.* I'll have that!'

Now read the text on the right-hand page. How does the text work with the illustration to build an atmosphere of suspense? What other words could describe how Bill approaches the box? What words could we use to explain how he is feeling?

Finally, take ideas about what could be in the box, before re-reading the final two lines and turning the page slowly to build anticipation.

Spread 4, ...baby!'

Did anybody guess that it was a baby in the box?

Stop after this line to focus on the illustration. What do the characters' expressions convey? What is common about the appearance of all three characters? (They are all wearing stripes.)

Continue reading the text and draw attention

to Bill's language, particularly his dialect. Can the children help Bill to speak 'proper'? (For example, *an* orphan rather than *a* orphan.) Notice his use of slang, such as 'grub'. Ask the children to share some slang words they know.

Point out the speech bubble in the second picture. Explain the difference between the way we show speech in text using speech marks and in illustrations using speech bubbles. Draw two speech bubbles on two pieces of paper. Write *yum yum* in one and *yuck* in the other. Ask a child to suggest an item of food for the baby and ask another member of the group to choose the speech bubble the baby would say in response.

Spread 5, Burglar Bill sits by the fire…

After reading the text, discuss how Burglar Bill tries to amuse the baby. Point out the repetition in the text. Why does the reader find this page amusing?

What does this spread tell us about Burglar Bill's character? Notice the speech bubble again and point out how the illustrator uses musical notation to show us that the words are being sung.

Spread 6, Burglar Bill bounces the baby…

Look at the comic strip illustrations and let the children discuss what is happening. Now read the text and point out that the author has used alliteration. Explain that this is when there is a string of words that use the same sound. Give an example ('Burglar Bill bounces the baby'), and ask the children for the dominant sound. Read the text again, asking the children to listen for more examples. Have fun with the full-length version of the Peter Piper tongue-twister. Ask the children for tongue-twisters they know, or see if you can create one as a group.

Spread 7, Burglar Bill plays with the baby…

The main interest of this spread is the contrast between the two illustrations. Invite the children to comment on them. Ask: *Would we know from the first picture that Bill was a burglar? How does this contrast with the night-time picture?* Read the text together and ask which sentence (notably under the second picture) reminds us that Bill is indeed a burglar.

Spread 8, At twelve o'clock…

Look at the illustrations before reading, and ask the children to use the pictorial cues to describe what is happening in each. Play 'spot the difference' between the two pictures.

Then read the text. Discuss how the author creates mood. Ask questions such as: *What image does 'snoring softly' create, and how? Which sentences create suspense? Why?*

Spread 9, Burglar Bill creeps…

Ask the children to look at Burglar Bill's body position in the picture, and to think of expressive words to describe his pose and actions.

Read the text, remembering to use a higher-pitched (female) voice than you do for Bill. Highlight how this voice echoes Bill's words and catchphrases. Focus on the last line of text. Why do the children think this is in capital letters? Would lower case convey the same feeling? Invite the children to try to show the difference with their voices.

Spread 10, There, with a black mask…

Cover the illustration before reading the text. Then reveal the picture and ask what common features identify both characters as burglars. This list might also include the fact that both their names begin with B. Would it work as well if their names didn't start with this sound? Ask the children to explain what the *Police Gazette* might be and what sort of things it might report on.

Talk about why the two burglars are able to sit down together and have cocoa and biscuits. Were the children surprised that the burglar was a woman? Explain the meaning of the word *stereotype* and elicit that we tend to think of burglars as men. Are there any other gender-based stereotypes that the children can think of (such as nurses usually thought of as women, firefighters as men)?

Spread 11, 'Oh, I got a baby,'

The text re-uses lots of phrases that the reader has read before. Betty echoes Bill's 'Well blow me down!' and there is much repetition of 'big brown box'. Draw attention to the capital letters that emphasise 'BROWN' and 'HOLES'. Write up this sentence on the board with emphasis on different words to play with the idea of how this writer's tool can change the meaning of the text.

Spread 12, Back in the kitchen…

Allow the children to enjoy the details in the illustrations. Do they recognise the kitchen scene from the first page? What are the main differences they notice? Can they detect how the illustrator has used colour to convey atmosphere?

How would the children describe a typical day in the life of Bill or Betty? Discuss ways in which Bill and Betty are similar. For example, their language is similar: 'I ain't'; 'when I come out'; 'I never knowed'.

What are the dominant themes in the story so far?

Can the children predict what the denouement of the story may be when Betty reveals that she

has no husband? Highlight this as a key moment when the author moves the story on.

Spread 13, Burglar Bill walks through the town…

The illustration here is a continuous spread across the double page. Can the children recall which other pages in the book were similar? (Spreads 3 and 9.) Discuss how this picture and that in spread 9 could both indicate a journey. Why do the children think Bill is looking back over his shoulder? After reading the text, point out that the journey could also be symbolic of the couple's journey towards enlightenment. Which sentences show that Bill and Betty finally see the error of their ways? Why has the author emphasised some words through the use of capital letters?

Spread 14, '…TAKE THEM BACK!'

Encourage the children to join in reading out the three words on this spread. Allow them to revel in the delightful detail of the illustrations. Discuss what items are being returned where and to whom.

Spread 15, So Burglar Bill…

Read the final page. Encourage the children to think about why Bill becomes a baker. Can they think of any other professions he might have been good at? Do any of these ideas begin with B? Point out how Bill and Betty teach the baby the same phrases they both use throughout the story.

Finish by asking the children to share their thoughts about the book. Which parts did they enjoy? Were there any parts they didn't like? How would they recommend this story to someone else?

Shared reading

Tues WK2

Extract 1

- Together with the class, read an enlarged copy of Extract 1.
- Highlight the 'ow' digraph in the words 'blow' and 'down'. Ask the children to read the words and identify the two different sounds made by 'ow'. Invite them to sort the following words into the two sound categories: 'flow', 'clown', 'grow', 'brow', 'slow', 'brown'. Can the children think of any other words that could be added to the lists?
- Point out the first set of dialogue in the extract and explain that speech marks are used to show the words that someone is speaking within a piece of text.
- Ask the children to help you underline all dialogue in the extract. Explain how speech can also be used in illustrations using a speech bubble, giving examples from the book.
- Re-read the extract and ask the children to identify any grammar that might not be considered correct. Can they explain why Bill might speak in this way? Talk about their suggestions.

Tues WK2

Extract 2

- Read an enlarged copy of Extract 2 with the children. Point out the alliteration in the first sentence. Underline the word 'knee' and ask the children to circle the 'ee' digraph. Look carefully at the blend 'kn'. Ask the children to identify which letter is silent and to suggest other words that contain this blend. Write these on the board and have some fun reading them with and without the silent 'k', covering and uncovering the first letter as you do this.
- Highlight the tongue-twister phrase and discuss what makes this sentence tricky to say. Teach the children the full tongue-twister. Then change the initial sound from 'p' to another consonant and repeat the tongue-twister. Does this make it easier to say?
- Look at the baby's pronunciation of Bill's name as 'Boglaboll'. Ask the children to try changing the vowel sounds in 'Burglar Bill' to make different versions of baby talk.

Extract 3

Fri WK2

- Read a copy of the enlarged text, modelling appropriate expression and intonation. Point out that the author builds suspense with the alternation between Burglar Bill creeping upstairs and Burglar Betty's chatter downstairs.
- Ask the children which word in this sequence focuses the atmosphere of suspense. ('creeps'.)
- Look at the long vowel phoneme in the word 'creeps'. Ask the children to circle the other long vowel phonemes in the extract that have the same sound. Highlight that there are two spellings of the sound. Can the children help you to compile lists of words which contain 'ea' and 'ee'?
- Underline the words 'date' and 'cake'. What similarities do the children notice about these words? Discuss the long vowel sound made by the split digraph 'ae'. Use three children with three letter cards ('a', 'e' and a consonant) to show how this works. Stand the 'a' and 'e' children together, then ask the other child to split up the 'ae' digraph with their consonant. Use a variety of consonants to make different words.
- Discuss why the author has written the final sentence in the extract in capital letters. Talk about the use of cliffhangers as a tool for creating suspense in books or drama.

Extract 1

'Blow me down,' he says. 'It ain't no police cars, it's a... baby!'

Burglar Bill puts the baby on the table.

'What was you doing in that box, baby?' he says.

But the baby only keeps on crying.

'All alone,' says Burglar Bill. He pats the baby's little hand. 'A orphan!'

Text extract and illustration © 1977, Janet and Allan Ahlberg.

Extract 2

Burglar Bill bounces the baby on his knee.

'So you can talk,' he says. 'Say "Burglar Bill".'

'Boglaboll,' says the baby.

'Say "Peter Piper picked a peck of pickled pepper",' says Burglar Bill.

'Boglaboll,' says the baby.

Suddenly Burglar Bill feels his knee getting wet and smells a smell.

'Poo,' he says. 'I know what YOU want!'

Text extract and illustrations © 1977, Janet and Allan Ahlberg.

Extract 3

Burglar Bill creeps to the top of the stairs. Down below a torch is shining and a voice says, 'That's a nice umbrella – I'll have that!'

Burglar Bill creeps down the stairs. The voice says, 'That's a nice tin of beans – I'll have that!'

Burglar Bill creeps along the hall and into the kitchen. The voice says, 'That's a nice date and walnut cake with buttercream filling and icing on the top – I'll have that!'

BURGLAR BILL PUTS ON THE LIGHT.

Text extract and illustration © 1977, Janet and Allan Ahlberg.

SCHOLASTIC
www.scholastic.co.uk

Plot, character and setting

Mon Wk1

Wanted!

> **Objective:** To write for a purpose, identifying and describing features of a character.
> **What you need:** Copies of *Burglar Bill*, copies of photocopiable page 15, pencils and colouring pencils.
> **Cross-curricular links:** Art and design, citizenship

What to do

● Read the first two spreads of the book. Ask the children to describe what sort of person they think Bill is from the description given of him so far.
● Explain that the children have been asked to put up some posters for the police to warn the public about this burglar and ask people for help in catching him.
● Establish the purpose of these posters. What information will the public need in order to recognise Burglar Bill?
● Allow time for the children to discuss in pairs or small groups what clues from the spreads they can use to make their judgements. Ask questions such as: *What does he look like? What might he be wearing? What has he stolen? What does he say? What does he have with him? How does he get into houses?* Talk about adjectives being used to describe things. Together record a list of descriptive words the children have used.
● Provide each child with a copy of photocopiable page 15. Tell the children that they can use this to design their 'Wanted!' posters. Explain that the headings will help them to construct the text of the poster.

> **Differentiation**
> **For older/more confident learners:** Challenge children to develop their descriptions into a poem about Burglar Bill.
> **For younger/less confident learners:** Allow children to discuss their illustration with you, so that you can scribe their descriptions for them.

Wed Wk2

Trial of the burglars

> **Objective:** To present a persuasive argument, drawing on knowledge of traditional tales.
> **What you need:** Copies of photocopiable page 16, copies of *Burglar Bill*, copies of the stories 'Goldilocks' and 'Jack and the Beanstalk' (ensure that the children are familiar with these stories), pencils.
> **Cross-curricular links:** Citizenship, drama

What to do

● Choose three children to act as Goldilocks, Jack and Burglar Bill. Divide the rest of the class into three groups.
● Explain to the groups that that they will have to decide whether Goldilocks, Jack and Burglar Bill are guilty of robbery. Assign a character to each group to focus on.
● Provide each group with a copy of photocopiable page 16 and assign a note-taker to complete it.
● Ask the groups to join with their characters. Tell them to read the questions in the first part of the sheet and discuss what they think their character might say in order to escape punishment.
● Once they have completed this part of the activity, bring the children back together and ask each group to present the questions to their character. Encourage the characters to answer according to the reasons agreed in their groups.
● Each group should then discuss the reasons for their chosen verdict and agree on a fitting punishment if relevant.
● As a whole class, discuss the verdicts and punishments and take feedback on the task. Ask questions such as: *Were any verdicts difficult to reach? If so, why? Were some punishments more severe than others? Why?*

> **Differentiation**
> **For older/more confident learners:** Challenge children to choose a character and record the 'trial' in the form of a court report.
> **For younger/less confident learners:** Provide support for their ideas to be scribed.

Plot, character and setting

I'll have that! *Wed Wk7*

> **Objective:** To use descriptive language including adjectives.
> **What you need:** Copies of *Burglar Bill*, a selection of familiar household objects (toothbrush, pair of slippers, magazine, box of teabags and so on).
> **Cross-curricular links:** Design and technology

What to do

- With the class, read pages 4 to 6 of the book (taking the title page as page 1), where Burglar Bill steals objects from houses.
- Ask the children if they can identify the significant language difference between 'That's a nice tin of beans' and 'That's a nice big brown box with little holes in it'. Elicit that in the latter sentence Bill uses adjectives to describe the object rather than just saying what it is. Write the two sentences on the board. Invite children to come up to highlight the adjectives.
- Ask the children to use their copies of the book to identify other stolen objects in Bill's house and then describe them in the same way that Bill described the box. (Ensure that the children understand that colours are also adjectives.)
- Now bring out your prop box and explain that you have a selection of items that Bill might like to steal. Invite one child to look inside the box and choose an item without showing it to the rest of the class. They should then describe the object using adjectives, but not reveal what it is – for example, 'a nice small thing with soft bristles and a long pink handle'.
- Ask the other children to use the description to work out what the item is (in this case, a toothbrush).

> **Differentiation**
> **For older/more confident learners:** Encourage the children to add extra detail about colour to each item on their list.
> **For younger/less confident learners:** Let the children draw the ingredients instead of writing them.

Beginning, middle, end

> **Objective:** To retell a story using an understanding of sequential story structure.
> **What you need:** Copies of *Burglar Bill*, copies of photocopiable page 17 (including a teacher's copy enlarged and cut into six cards), Blu-Tack or similar.
> **Cross-curricular link:** Numeracy

What to do

- Read the quote on one of the cards and ask the children to find the page it comes from in the book. Establish whether it is found towards the beginning, middle or end of the story, and position the card appropriately on the board. Repeat this exercise with two more cards.
- Challenge the children to place the remaining three cards within the sequence on the board.
- Now explain to the children that you would like them to think about connective words and phrases that indicate the passing of time across the cards (such as 'Every night', 'Suddenly', 'After a while'). Write some suggestions on the board.
- Explore the book to find examples of time passing ('Just then', 'From now on', 'When spring comes' and so on). Ask the children to help you retell the story using the cards as cues.
- Now ask the children to close their eyes while you move one or two cards out of sequence. Tell them to open their eyes and read the cards. Can they say what is wrong with the sequence? Can they retell the story as it is? Discuss whether it still makes sense.
- Challenge the children to put the cards back in the right order using the language 'beginning', 'middle' and 'end' as they explain what they are doing.

> **Differentiation**
> **For older/more confident learners:** Ask children to tell you a different story (such as a well-known fairy tale), relating events in the correct sequence.
> **For younger/less confident learners:** Allow children to draw illustrations to sequence the story.

Contrasting settings

Objective: To compare story settings, exploring how setting contributes to atmosphere.
What you need: Copies of *Burglar Bill*, large sheets of paper, pencils.

What to do
● Allow the children time to examine the illustrations on page 3, where Bill is fast asleep in bed, and on the double-page spread where Bill and Betty are creeping through the town.
● Encourage the children to comment on similarities or differences they can see.
● Ask them to suggest descriptive words or phrases that paint a word-picture of each setting. Record these ideas on the board.
● Divide the class into two and allocate one of the two illustrations to each group. Challenge the groups to identify the key features in the setting and record these pictorially on a large sheet of paper.

● Give the children time to accompany their sketches with some words that describe how atmosphere is created in the illustration. Guide them to describe possible smells, sounds, textures and other sensory experiences as well as characters' thoughts or feelings.
● Bring the children back together to share ideas. Discuss what effect the illustrations have on the story. Would reading the text alone convey these images and create the same atmosphere?

Differentiation
For older/more confident learners: Let children choose another picture or section of text that illustrates how setting is important to the story. Ask them to explain their choice in a paragraph or two.
For younger/less confident learners: Ask children to choose a picture that shows how setting is important to the story. Help them to write a list of descriptive words about the setting. Record their ideas on large sheets of paper, annotating their responses.

The big brown box

Objective: To make predictions and create alternative storylines.
What you need: Photocopiable page 18, pencils, a brown cardboard box containing a collection of objects that have a distinctive texture (such as a sponge, teabag, bag of cooked pasta, bag of dry pasta, feathers, pine cone).
Cross-curricular links: Drama

What to do
● Hide your collection of objects inside the big brown box. Provide each child with a copy of photocopiable page 18.
● Invite a volunteer to close their eyes (or wear a blindfold), and tell them to feel what's inside the box. Ask them to pick one item and describe what they can feel, without revealing what they think the object is. Tell the other children to use the photocopiable sheet to write down the descriptive words used by the speaker and suggest

what they think the object is. Then ask the child to open their eyes, take out the object and reveal it. Continue with other volunteers and objects.
● Ask the children to think of an object that Bill might have found in the box instead of a baby. Lead them to think of an item that would inspire an interesting story – perhaps an animal of some sort, some jewels, a rare painting, an airline ticket. Ask them to think about how the plot of this alternative story would develop.

Differentiation
For older/more confident learners: Challenge the children to write an account of what might happen when Burglar Bill opens the box and finds an alternative object.
For younger/less confident learners: Ask the children to draw the new object in the box. Play 'Kim's game' using objects in the box. Encourage the use of descriptive language.

Plot, character and setting

+ Tues WK1

Burglar dance

> **Objective:** To explore how suspense is created in a text.
> **What you need:** Copies of *Burglar Bill*, paper, pencils, two pieces of contrasting music (one that has a dark, ominous feel to it, such as John Williams' theme from *Jaws*, and the other a light-hearted piece, such as *Baby Elephant Walk* by Henry Mancini).
> **Cross-curricular links:** PE (dance), music

What to do

● Re-read the book, asking the children to identify sentences that convey Burglar Bill's movement. These include mentions of creeping, climbing, falling, swinging, bouncing and running. Write these movement words and phrases on the board.

● Play the recording of the creepy-sounding music and ask the children to think about which movement descriptions fit best to this music. Encourage them to make freeze-frame body shapes to illustrate the movements mentioned on the board. Help the children to put some of these movements to the music.

● Now repeat this activity using the jolly piece of music.

● Gather the children together again to discuss how words in the text are carefully put together to create a mood. Ask: *What would happen if there were no descriptive movement words? What would happen if you substituted certain descriptive words for different words?* (For example, stagger, jump.) *Does it change the dance?*

> **Differentiation**
> **For older/more confident learners:** Allow time for children to put their movements together to make a sequence and to perform their dance with gesture and facial expression.
> **For younger/less confident learners:** Model a variety of movements and actions for children to practise.

? Tues WK2

'The error of my ways'

> **Objective:** To give reasons for events in a story or changes in characters.
> **What you need:** Copies of *Burglar Bill*, paper, pencils.

What to do

● Working in pairs, ask the children to read the spread beginning 'Burglar Bill walks through the town...'. Ask them to discuss what the statement 'I can see the error of my ways' might mean. What do they think has caused the two burglars to come to this realisation?

● Encourage the children to think about how other famous storybook characters might change their behaviour if they were to see the error of their ways. Record on the board the names of characters who do bad things in fairy tales.

● Ask the children to regroup into their pairs and choose a character, thinking of ways that character might change their behaviour. What would they do to make amends?

● Return as a class and invite the children to present their ideas using the following question-and-answer format:
    Child A: '[Character name], what have you done wrong?'
    Child B answers in character.
    Child A: 'And do you see the error of your ways?'
    Child B: 'I do. From now on I will...'

● Ask the children whether they think their character feels happier now he has decided to change. What do they think the consequences of Burglar Bill changing his behaviour have been?

> **Differentiation**
> **For older/more confident learners:** Challenge the children to write a new ending to their character's story, incorporating their ideas of character reformation.
> **For younger/less confident learners:** Children could tape-record their ideas in a pair or group discussion.

WANTED!

Burglar Bill

Description _____

_____

_____

Stolen item _____

_____

Useful information _____

_____

Reward _____

Plot, character and setting

Trial of the burglars

Questions for the accused hereby charged with the crime of burglary

- What is your name?

  Response: _____

- What were you doing in the victim's house?

  Response: _____

- What reasons did you have to take the items?

  Response: _____

  _____

- How have you changed your ways?

  Response: _____

  _____

- How do you plead? Guilty or not guilty?

  Response: _____

Verdict: Guilty/Not guilty
If guilty, does the accused deserve a punishment?
If so, what?

Beginning, middle, end

He has stolen fish and chips.	'Sounds like TWO police cars!'
'Poo,' he says. 'I know what YOU want!'	Downstairs there is a noise.
Burglar Betty tells him how she lost the baby.	'I can see the error of my ways,' says Burglar Bill.

Text © 1977, Allan Ahlberg.

The big brown box

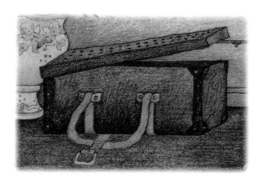

Descriptive words	What do you think it is?
Item 1	
Item 2	
Item 3	
Item 4	
Item 5	
Item 6	

Illustration © 1977, Janet Ahlberg.

Talk about it

Fn wk1

The same or different?

Objective: To consider moral issues around a story's ideas, events and characters.
What you need: Photocopiable page 22, pencils.
Cross-curricular links: PSHE, citizenship

What to do
● Tell the children to look carefully at the two pictures on photocopiable page 22. Allow some silent thinking time, then ask them to jot down any similarities and differences between the two characters, giving reasons for these decisions.
● Gather the children into a circle. Remind them about good listening and respect for others. Ask them to share the similarities and differences that they found, and reasons why. Extend the discussion by modelling questions such as:
1. Why did Goldilocks and Burglar Bill steal things? Did Goldilocks and Bill steal for the same reason?

2. Goldilocks is only a child. Is it any different if children steal?
3. What is stealing? Can stealing ever be right? What makes something yours?
4. What does punishment mean? Were Burglar Bill and Goldilocks punished?
5. Were Goldilocks and Burglar Bill sorry about what they had done? Is saying sorry the same thing as being sorry? Does saying sorry help you feel better?

Differentiation
For older/more confident learners: Encourage the children to agree/disagree with the opinions of others, giving reasons why. Tell them to think beyond the appearance of another fictional character and to think about actions or behaviour.
For younger/less confident learners: In pairs, ask the children to discuss their ideas about the questions posed. Provide adult support to scribe ideas.

Would you rather?

? Thurs wk2 then writing sequel to story – Burglar Bill wasn't happy working in the bakery so he decided to became a burglar again.

Objective: To use talk to organise, sequence and clarify thinking, decision making, ideas and feelings.
What you need: An enlarged copy of photocopiable page 23, cut into four; a large sheet of paper to record children's ideas; space large enough for children to move around in and form a circle.
Cross-curricular link: Philosophy

What to do
● Gather the children together in the large space. Explain that they are going to have to make a choice between four objects that Burglar Bill could steal.
● Hold up and read the cards from photocopiable page 23. Place each one in a different corner of the floor space.
● Ask the children to stand by the card that they think Burglar Bill would choose. Emphasise that they must make one choice only.
● There should be, hopefully, several children to each card, thus forming a group. Encourage

each group to discuss why they have chosen that particular object.
● Now invite the children to sit down in their groups. Start a class discussion by asking one member of a group why they chose that particular item. Encourage children from other groups to question the choices of others or say why they did not choose that item. You may need to model this to begin with. Repeat this activity with each group.
● Now let children move to a different card if they wish. Ask those who move to explain what changed their thinking.

Differentiation
For older/more confident learners: Encourage the children to build on the ideas of others by referring to statements made previously.
For younger/less confident learners: Ensure that less confident speakers are given support to share their ideas within the safety of the small group.

Talk about it

Good or bad?

Objective: To explore characters' behaviour, giving reasons for ideas.
What you need: *Burglar Bill*, two shoeboxes (one labelled 'good', the other 'bad'), paper, pencils.
Cross-curricular links: PSHE, citizenship

What to do
● Tell the children to write their name on a sheet of paper. Then ask them to decide whether Burglar Bill is a good person or a bad person. Once they have made their choice, they should put their piece of paper in either the box labelled 'good' or the one labelled 'bad'.
● Empty the boxes one at a time and record on the board who made which choice.
● Invite children to explain the reasons for their choice. Ensure everyone has a chance to speak.

● Ask questions that prompt deeper thinking about what makes a person good or bad. For example: *Can a good person do something bad? Can a bad person do something good? Who decides what is good or bad?*
● Now hand back the name cards and invite the children to vote again on whether they think Burglar Bill is good or bad. Look at the results. Has anyone changed their mind? If so, why?

Differentiation
For older/more confident learners: Repeat the task for Burglar Betty. Are the reasons different? Who do the children think is better, Bill or Betty? Why?
For younger/less confident learners: Model examples of responses, such as: *Is it because...? Can you think of a reason already given that you agree with?*

Concept line

Objective: To use talk to organise, sequence and clarify thinking; interact with others and justify ideas.
What you need: *Burglar Bill*, a brown box with little holes in it, a long piece of string (or skipping rope), two cards, A5 paper, blank labels, pencils.
Cross-curricular links: Philosophy, PSHE

What to do
● Discuss as a class why the baby is the most important thing in the world to Betty and Bill.
● Show the children the brown box. Explain that inside it is a very important thing. Ask the children to write their name on a piece of paper and draw a large outline of the box. They should then write or draw what they think is inside the box. Explain that they will then try to decide as a class the level of importance for each item through allocating it a place on the concept line.
● Lay out the piece of string/rope. At one end place a card saying 'most important', and at the other a card saying 'least important'.
● Tell the children to place their papers in the box. Invite volunteers, one by one, to pick a paper from the box, read it out and place it on the line.

● Allow some discussion about where the papers have been placed. Is there any disagreement? Why? The objects can be moved if explanations can be justified and the majority agree.
● Ask children to explain and interpret their drawings of the most important thing. Ask: *What does that object mean to you?* Perhaps 'my mum' could match the concept of love, and 'treasure' could mean wealth. Remind the children that there is usually a reason why we want objects in our lives. This reason could be a big idea such as love, hate, power, happiness, revenge, greed and so on. Write labels for concepts offered.
● Ask the children to decide which labels best fit their choices, and to add the concept labels to their drawings. Ask: *Do the labels change where objects should be placed? Why?* The children may move objects on the line if they can justify why.

Differentiation
For older/more confident learners: Encourage children to make their own set of concept cards.
For younger/less confident learners: Help children by suggesting concepts based on their explanations.

Talk about it

Questions and themes

Objective: To listen to other viewpoints and work effectively as a group, challenging, supporting and moving on.
What you need: Copies of *Burglar Bill*, a set of theme cards from an enlarged copy of photocopiable page 24, paper, pencils.
Cross-curricular links: PSHE, citizenship

What to do
● Ask the children to think about the events of the story. Explain that they will be connecting these events to some theme cards.
● Show the cards and explain briefly what each card means. Ask the children which themes are in the story and to give an example from the text. Discard any themes that the children do not think occur in the story.
● Now ask the children to think of or write down a question about the story that connects to one or more of the themes. For the theme of 'theft', for example, they could ask: *Why do Burglar Bill and Betty take back the things they stole?*
● Gather the children into a circle. Record the questions and the related theme on a large sheet of paper or the board.
● Invite the children to vote on one of the questions to talk about. Lead the discussion to develop the main idea. Ensure that the children give reasons to support their responses.
● Ask the children to summarise the main themes in *Burglar Bill*. Have further questions been raised from their discussion?

Differentiation
For older/more confident learners: Ask children to list reasons why they think certain themes appear in the story. Can they think of other story themes?
For younger/less confident learners: Ask children to practise putting questions to a partner. Model the use of the word 'Why', relating questions to the story.

News broadcast: returned items

Objective: To take into account the needs of the listener and include relevant information when speaking for a purpose.
What you need: Copies of *Burglar Bill*, a large box made to look like a television with cut-out screen, clipboards, paper, pencils, hats, props and microphones (optional).
Cross-curricular links: Drama, ICT

What to do
● Explain to the children that they are going to produce a news broadcast about the story that some stolen goods have been mysteriously returned to the owners.
● Put the children into pairs. Explain that one partner should take the role of the reporter and the other should act as a resident of the town where Burglar Bill lives.
● Encourage the pairs to recall the stolen goods that were returned. They should then think of possible questions that a reporter would ask the resident. Offer examples such as: *When did you realise your toothbrush was missing / had been returned? Did you hear or see anything strange during the night?* The 'resident' should think of answers to the reporter's questions.
● Give practice time before inviting the pairs to perform their broadcasts behind the television screen. Remind them to use clear voices.
● After each performance, encourage the rest of the class to give feedback. Was enough information given about the burglaries? Was the report clear about how the items re-appeared?

Differentiation
For older/more confident learners: Challenge the children to write the report in the form of a script and to record the interview using a video camera.
For younger/less confident learners: Develop this activity through role play. Provide props and materials for children to build role-play areas such as a television studio or police interview room.

The same or different?

Burglar Bill   Goldilocks

The same because…

Different because…

Illustration of Burglar Bill © 1977, Janet Ahlberg. Illustration of Goldilocks © 2009, Shelagh McNicholas.

Talk about it

Would you rather?

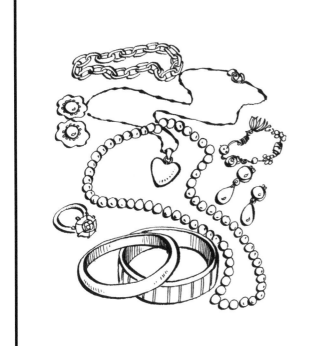

Jewels

Money

Toys

Kitten

Illustration © 2009, Shelagh McNicholas.

Questions and themes

Fairness

Happiness

Guilt

Fear

Theft

Knowledge

Love

Honesty

Get writing

Mon wk2

Writing a blurb

> **Objective:** To summarise a plot and write simple
> sentences independently.
> **What you need:** Copies of *Burglar Bill*, paper,
> pencils.
> **Cross-curricular link:** Art and design

What to do

● Look at the back cover of the book and read
the blurb together.

● Explain that books have a blurb to help
someone discover a bit about the book's plot
before they read it. Discuss what would make a
reader choose a book, and why. Tell the children
that they will be writing their own *Burglar Bill*
blurb in this lesson.

● Explore the format of the blurb. What do
the children notice? Elicit that there are four
questions followed by an answer. Look at the
question format and use of the word 'who'. Ask

the children to help you make a list of other
question words.

● Allow the children time to look through the
book to find information they could use in their
own blurb. Then let them design and illustrate
their own back covers. They should choose a
question word to use in their blurb and use the
original structure (questions and the answer
'It's Burglar Bill').

● Tell the children to read their blurbs to each
other, asking if their blurb would encourage
them to choose the book.

> **Differentiation**
> **For older/more confident learners:** Challenge
> children to use interesting adverbs and adjectives to
> make the blurb descriptive.
> **For younger/less confident learners:** Limit the
> sentence structure to one or two questions. Provide
> a bank of useful words.

Speaking 'proper'

> **Objective:** To use phonic knowledge to read and
> write simple words and show an understanding of
> correct grammar.
> **What you need:** A copy of photocopiable page 28 for
> each child, pencils, copies of *Burglar Bill*.

What to do

● As you read the story, ask the children to listen
out for any words, phrases or sentences that do
not sound quite right and are not grammatically
correct.

● Take suggestions (for example, 'What was you
doing in that box, baby?') and record these on
the board. Point out that all the examples are
contained in the dialogue.

● Ask the children why Burglar Bill and Burglar
Betty might speak this way. Do they know
anyone who uses dialect? Can they think of any

television programmes where characters speak
with strong accents?

● Ask the children to tell you why they think the
baby's words are different. Explain that the baby
can only pronounce some of the sounds. Which
sounds do the children think a baby might find
easiest to make?

● Provide each child with a copy of the
photocopiable sheet and ask them to rewrite the
words, phrases and sentences correctly.

> **Differentiation**
> **For older/more confident learners:** Challenge
> children to rewrite a prose section of the book as if
> Burglar Bill were reading it out loud, using accent
> and intonation.
> **For younger/less confident learners:** Write a list of
> words and suggest that the children translate them
> into baby words using the dominant sounds.

Get writing

Baby care manual

> **Objective:** To use instructional language and convey information in a non-narrative form.
> **What you need:** Copies of photocopiable page 29, *Burglar Bill*, a variety of instruction texts, pencils.

What to do

● Look together at some of the examples of instructional writing. Ask the children to explain the difference between a story and this form of text. Elicit that instructional writing tells the reader how to do something, such as make a meal, as in a recipe book.

● Explain to the children that they are going to help you write a manual for Burglar Bill so that he will know how to look after the baby.

● Look through *Burglar Bill* together. What things does Bill need help with? (Changing nappies, feeding, stopping the baby from crying, entertaining the baby, making sleeping arrangements.)

● Together, think about which words might be useful to a reader trying to follow instructions in order (for example *first, next, finally*).

● Model step-by-step instructions on how to eat cereal. Ask the children for feedback. What did they notice? Did the instructions make sense? What would happen if the steps were in a different order?

● Hand out copies of the photocopiable sheet. Ask the children to cut out the pictures and stick them on a larger piece of paper in the correct order; they should write an instructional caption underneath each picture with your support.

> **Differentiation**
> **For older/more confident learners:** Challenge children to design and illustrate a manual on a subject of their own choice.
> **For younger/less confident learners:** Act as scribe for the children, captioning the pictures with instructional words they suggest.

Stolen items

> **Objective:** To write a list of objects, using imagination.
> **What you need:** A carrier bag, large outline drawings of two sacks (one labelled 'Betty's swag' and the other 'Bill's swag'), four short strips of paper for each child, writing materials.

What to do

● Let the children look at the drawings of the swag bags. Can anyone explain what they are? Elicit that 'swag' is a slang word for stolen goods.

● Challenge the children to think of two things that Bill might like to steal and two things that Betty might steal. Discuss briefly a few examples of items that different genders might choose, and why. Tell the children to use their imaginations and not divulge their ideas to others.

● Allow time for the children to write each of their ideas on one of the strips of paper provided, then collect the strips in the carrier bag.

● Shake the bag and ask the children to come up one at a time to pick and read out a strip of paper. The child should then decide whose swag bag the item belongs in, and why. Write each item inside the appropriate sack drawing.

● Discuss how a list is displayed. (Each item placed below the previous one.) Why do the children think a list is written in this way? Discuss when you might tick or cross items off a list.

● Ask: *Can you think of other occasions when people might need to write a list? Why?* (Shopping lists, 'to do' lists, class registration, recipes, instruction manuals and so on.)

> **Differentiation**
> **For older/more confident learners:** Challenge children to look through the book and compile a list of everything they think might have been stolen.
> **For younger/less confident learners:** Ask children to draw a swag bag with one of Bill's stolen items and another bag for one of Betty's items. Help them to use their phonetic knowledge to label the two items.

Get writing

Take them back

> **Objective:** To write for various purposes, using features of different forms such as lists, using phonetic knowledge to spell unfamiliar words.
> **What you need:** Photocopiable page 30 for each child, copies of *Burglar Bill*, sticky notes, pencils.

What to do

● Remind the children that Burglar Bill and Burglar Betty have decided to return all the stolen items to their original owners. Explain that they have forgotten, however, which item belongs to which person, so the children are going to help Bill and Betty by labelling the objects.

● Encourage the children to tell you where they have seen examples of labels and what purpose they had (such as price tags on products to buy, food labels, luggage labels).

● Give each child a sticky note and ask them to write on it the name of a stolen object from the story (for example, mug, toothbrush, goldfish, hat, helmet, umbrella, piano, stuffed fish).

● Place one of the labels on a child's back. (The child should not know what their label reads.) Tell the child to sit at the front of the class and ask questions of the rest of the children to ascertain what stolen item is written on their label.

● Now ask the children to look at the illustrations on the photocopiable sheet. Their task is to help Bill and Betty describe each object and so help them identify who it might belong to. Ask them to name the item, write two words that describe it and suggest who the item might belong to.

● Share some of the children's descriptions and see if the rest of the class can guess who they might belong to.

> **Differentiation**
> **For older/more confident learners:** Ask children to look through *Burglar Bill* and pick out other objects in Bill's house to label.
> **For younger/less confident learners:** Provide children with five or six items (toothbrush, comb, clock and so on). Help them to write a label to name each item.

Bakery Bill

> **Objective:** To convey information in a non-narrative form.
> **What you need:** Recipes in books/magazines that include pictures of cakes/buns/biscuits, coloured pencils, paper, sugar paper, internet access (optional).
> **Cross-curricular links:** Science, Design & technology

What to do

● Look together at some recipes for tea-time treats. Explain the form and purpose of a recipe. Ask the children to share any experiences they have of baking or cooking.

● Read one of your example recipes and discuss the ingredients and method. Was the recipe easy to follow and understand?

● Explain that Burglar Bill will need to learn to cook if he is to succeed in his new job as baker. To help him, the children are going to compile a recipe book of simple cakes, buns and biscuits.

● Model the creation of an interesting recipe, demonstrating the format on the board.

● Organise the children into pairs and give them a simple recipe to find (such as flapjacks, fairy cakes, muffins), using the internet, recipe books and magazines. Tell each pair to write out the recipe in their own words and choice of layout, and to illustrate it. Write useful headings on the board: 'Ingredients', 'Method', 'What you need'.

● The completed recipes can be collated and stuck into a book ready to give to Bakery Bill!

> **Differentiation**
> **For older/more confident learners:** Ask children to write a more creative recipe, such as Surprise banana buns or Fizz-bang biscuits. Encourage them to include weights and measures in their recipe too.
> **For younger/less confident learners:** Let children simply draw the steps and label the main ingredients.

Speaking 'proper'

Incorrect grammar	Translation/correction
'It ain't no police car'	
'What was you doing in that box?'	
'grub'	
'Runfrit!'	
'all them things'	

■SCHOLASTIC
www.scholastic.co.uk

READ & RESPOND: Activities based on Burglar Bill

Baby care manual

How to feed beans to a baby in six easy steps

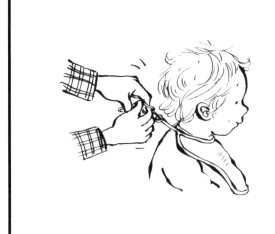

Illustration © 2009, Shelagh McNicholas.

Take them back

● Look at the pictures below. Label them.

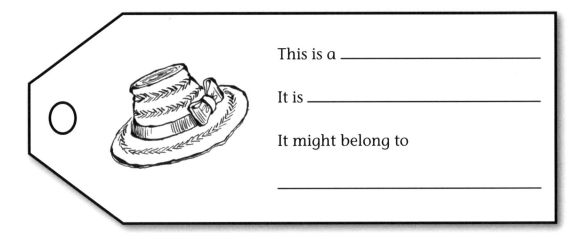

This is a _____

It is _____

It might belong to

_____

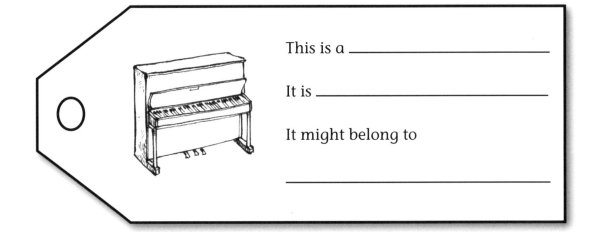

This is a _____

It is _____

It might belong to

_____

This is a _____

It is _____

It might belong to

_____

READ & RESPOND: Activities based on Burglar Bill

SCHOLASTIC
www.scholastic.co.uk

Illustration © 2009, Shelagh McNicholas.

Assessment

Assessment advice

Burglar Bill is full of opportunities for children to engage meaningfully with the story. Its strong narrative inspires children to get involved with the actions, choices and consequences of the characters' behaviours. Janet Ahlberg's illustrations and Allan's words combine to make this a book especially suited to 'thinking for talking'. It is the children's thinking that leads to understanding and with this understanding comes empathy, expressiveness, energy and moral engagement. All these build strong foundations for further reading and writing.

The activities in this book encourage children to sequence events, offer comment and opinion, to justify behaviours and explore intentions. This book also challenges children to think in a rigorous and increasingly philosophical way. When children are encouraged to talk, think and listen together, we, as educators, are empowering them to make differences; to lead rather than be content to follow; to listen with respect and develop a social conscience.

Assessing what children believe about the book provides a thorough insight into their understanding of the text. Through listening to their ideas we can make sound judgements about what the children think as well as what they have learned.

Agree/disagree

Fri WK2

> **Assessment focus:** To show an understanding of the elements of stories, such as main character and sequence of events; to give reasons why things happen or characters change.
> **What you need:** Photocopiable page 32 for each child, pencils, two large cards (one labelled 'agree' and one labelled 'disagree'), large space to move around in.

What to do

● Provide each child with a copy of photocopiable page 32. Explain that you would like them to spend some silent time reflecting on the book. Read out the statements on the sheet.

● Show the children the agree/disagree cards and confirm their meaning. For example: *Agree is when you think the same, and disagree is when you think differently.*

● Ask the children to read the statements to themselves and tick the appropriate boxes on the photocopiable sheet. They should also write a brief sentence to explain their choice. Make it clear to

the children that at this stage these thoughts must be their own and they must not allow others to see their answers. Use this opportunity to explain that there are no right or wrong answers, as long as the children can back up their answers with a reason.

● When the sheets have been completed, ask the children to gather together. Place the 'agree' card on the floor in one area and the 'disagree' card a short distance away. Read one of the statements and ask the children to move quickly to the card that corresponds to the answer on their assessment sheet.

● Encourage individual children to explain to the group why they made that decision. Invite feedback and contrasting opinions from other children.

● Repeat this activity until all the children have had the chance to share their thoughts. If you discover that there are divided opinions, encourage the children to explore and discuss the different reasons given.

Agree/disagree

	agree	disagree

Burglar Bill was a bad man.

agree	disagree

Because _____

_____

Burglar Betty was a good mother.

agree	disagree

Because _____

_____

Burglar Bill did not deserve to be burgled.

agree	disagree

Because _____

_____

Burglar Bill looked after the baby well.

agree	disagree

Because _____

_____

Bill and Betty were truly sorry for their actions.

agree	disagree

Because _____

_____

■SCHOLASTIC
www.scholastic.co.uk

READ & RESPOND: Activities based on Burglar Bill